Super Scripts

Walking wi   3

Ben Myers

T

Published in 2002 by:
Nelson Thornes Ltd
Delta Place
27 Bath Road
CHELTENHAM
GL53 7TH
United Kingdom

02 03 04 05 06 / 10 9 8 7 6 5 4 3 2 1

A catalogue record for this book is available from the British Library

ISBN 0-7847-6514-X

Cover illustration by Stuart Williams
Page make-up by Tech-Set Ltd

Printed and bound in Croatia by Zrinski

Application for permission for public performance of this play must be made to Nelson Thornes Ltd.

D E D I C A T I O N

For Wendy Sherwood

Who taught me English at St Bartholomew's School in Newbury when I was twelve. In a short space of time she was a huge influence, and made me believe in my writing. I moved to Australia in 1989, and when I returned in 1992 it was to find that she had fought bravely, but ultimately lost a battle against leukaemia. So this is for Miss Sherwood, who once said I would have something published before I was fifteen.

It's a bit late Miss, but I hope you like it.

C O N T E N T S

INTRODUCTION

SuperScripts

SuperScripts is a series of plays for use in the English classroom and the Drama studio. The plays have been written by professional writers who share a delight in live performance and the challenges it offers actors, designers, directors and, of course, audiences.

Most of the plays in the series were written for professional companies but all are included because they tell stories and use techniques which will interest, excite and offer new insights to young people who are just coming to understand how drama works as an art form.

The range of plays in the series addresses the requirement to give students at Key Stages 3 and 4 an opportunity to study a variety of dramatic genres. The fact that they were all written for performance (and have indeed all been performed) means that they will also offer students the chance to understand how and why playscripts are different from novels. The Activities section which follows the play itself is designed to draw attention to this and extend students' abilities in reading, writing and of course performing drama.

Many of the activities invite students to use practical work to engage directly with the text or formulate their own creative responses to its form and content. Others focus on the importance of discussing, writing and designing. Both English and Drama specialists will find the series a valuable resource on which to draw in order to promote dramatic literacy. Of course, simply performing the plays wouldn't be a bad thing either!

WALKING WITH SHADOWS

It seems strange that while psychological thrillers are enormously popular in the cinema, few tend to appear as plays. The essential ingredients of the genre combine a fast-moving storyline, the threat of something horrible happening and an element of the supernatural. The protagonist of the psychological thriller is very often a young person. In dramatic terms, their vulnerability heightens the tension and creates a greater concern for them in the audience. The commonly accepted notion that young people, especially young women, are more prone to supernatural experiences makes the storyline more believable. Add to this the struggle that most young people face in sorting out the relationship between what is real and what is not, who they are and how others see them and how far they are in control of their own lives, and we begin to see why the psychological thriller has such an appeal to young audiences. You will doubtless also see why, when I first heard about a new play for young people called *Walking with Shadows*, I was immediately keen to both go and see it performed and get hold of the script.

I wasn't disappointed. *Walking with Shadows* is certainly a fast-moving play. Not only was I completely hooked when I saw it performed by a young cast at the Watermill Theatre in Newbury, I also found myself turning the pages of the script ever more quickly when Ben Myers sent me a revised version of it – even though I knew the ending already! Like all good thrillers, *Walking with Shadows* is driven by an internal logic that at once engages yet confounds us. Strange things happen and though we never discover exactly why, we have no trouble believing that, in the context of the narrative, they are inevitable. What Ben Myers achieves particularly in the play is to capture the voices of his teenage characters so well that the audience moves from initially questioning the real nature of Lorna Moon's troubled mind, to accepting that something above and beyond the normal is indeed happening to her. Finally, and chillingly, the play carries a sting in its tail that suggests things are not quite finished …!

Ben Myers says that his main aim in writing the play was to try and say something about what it's like to be a teenager 'before I forgot completely what it meant to be one'. Ideas for the play came from a series of workshops which explored the sort of feelings and issues that prey on teenage minds and make young people vulnerable. Ultimately, the workshops began to focus on a few unsettling questions which Ben summarises like this: 'Is there anything more truly terrifying than feeling completely and utterly isolated? Where do you turn when you feel alone? What voices do you hear? These are questions you may never ask until you find yourself in that situation and then all you want to do is escape them. We decided to pose these questions, peel back the layers and explore the darkness … When you are alone, in your darkest moments, what do you see?'

WALKING WITH SHADOWS

CAST LIST

LORNA	a 15 year old girl
CHRIS	a new guy in school
JAMIE	Lorna's younger brother
LORNA'S MUM	
LORNA'S DAD	
THE GIRL	
KATIE	Lorna's friends
SAL	
RICKY	
LUCY	Lorna's classmates but perhaps not her friends!
CONNOR	
BAZ	
ROBYN	
SARAH	
MARCUS	
MR BARNESS	Lorna's next-door neighbour
DR LANE	a psychiatrist
MISS FRENCH	an English Teacher
MDM BLANC	a French teacher
THE SHADOW CHORUS	

The first production of *Walking with Shadows* was performed at The Watermill Theatre, Newbury in July 2001. The cast included: Aimee Stones, Chris Smith, Constance Frost, Jenny Clarke, Oliver Ford-Lane, William Richardson, Hannah Medlam, Alison Pettafor, Lukas Medlam, Josie Glover, Joseph Walton, Jonathan Munro, Tom Ross, Harriet Titmus, Nicola Rae, Alice Howard, Rosie Hunt, Rachael O'Brien, Charlotte Smith, Eleanor Ware.

ACT ONE

SCENE ONE THE CATHARSIS

*The **Shadow Chorus**, perhaps masked and dressed to blend in with the set, are on stage as the audience enter. They are completely still. Lighting is dimmed, and there is a circle of playing cards set up centre stage, as in clockwork patience.*

SHADOW 1	When you are alone, in your darkest moments …
SHADOW 2	What do you see?
SHADOW 3	Whatever it is, you don't see me.
SHADOW 4	But I am there.
SHADOW 5	I speak with your voice.

***Shadows** begin to come to life.*

SHADOW 1	I breathe with your breath.
SHADOW 2	And I see with your eyes. And in your mind …
SHADOW 3	I play out the torment that gives me life.
SHADOW 4	But I am not the shadows of your mind.
SHADOW 5	If I were you would not see me.
SHADOW 1	If I were you would feel …
SHADOW 2	The pain of loss …
ALL SHADOWS	That she feels.

*Stage lights brighten. A girl enters. She sits centre stage and starts playing clockwork patience. She is **Lorna Moon**. The **Shadow Chorus** begin to sing to the tune of 'Ring a ring a roses'.*

SHADOWS	Ring a ring a roses
	A pocket full of posies
	Atishoo, atishoo
	We all fall down

*As she reaches the end of her game, **Lorna** explodes in apparent catharsis. The silhouette of a **Girl** appears in **Lorna's** mirror and observes her silently.*

Down where hope is silent

With fear your brow is crowned

Behind you, behind you

We'll drag you down

Shadows in the darkness

Shadows in the mind

We'll find you, we'll find you

Don't ever look behind.

***Lorna** reacts as if she can sense something behind her but as she turns the **Girl** is gone. **Lorna** approaches the mirror suspiciously. Lights fade to blackout.*

SCENE TWO PLAYGROUND MAFIA

*Stage lights brighten. Sound of a school bell ringing. School children cross the stage as though on a break. **Lorna** is sitting contemplating her lunch. **Ricky** comes over.*

RICKY Hey Lorna.

LORNA Hi Ricky. Have you seen Sal, she sent me a text, said she had some news?

RICKY Like what?

***Lorna** throws her sandwiches away.*

Hey, what was that?

LORNA Just my lunch ... *(defensively)* I didn't like the sandwiches, what?

RICKY Do you want some chocolate?

LORNA Do you know how many calories are in that?

RICKY Just enough to keep me alive until dinner. There's Sal and Katie.

Sal and *Katie* run over, excited.

SAL Hey guys, have you heard yet?

RICKY Heard what?

KATIE That's a no then.

SAL Major drama guys – Sarah Hartley and Marcus Clarke broke up …

KATIE Right in the middle of art …

SAL … total public humiliation!

RICKY Wow, so Sarah Hartley's in the market for a real man at last?

KATIE Let us know if you see any eh, short arse!

RICKY Listen Katie …

Lorna interrupts, waving him to silence.

LORNA Come on guys, what happened? Spill.

SAL That's a point – you do art. Where were you?

LORNA I didn't feel well.

KATIE What, again?

LORNA God, I get ill like twice and everyone gets stressed. Just get on with the story.

SAL OK, OK. Well, we're doing some sketching and Mr Cartwright has gone out for some reason. And Marcus is talking to Robyn Scott.

RICKY She's nice too …

KATIE Shut up Ricky. Anyway, they weren't just talking. More like flirting.

SAL So Marcus is all like 'Ooh what a great picture. You're really good'. Of course, Sarah doesn't like this at all …

KATIE I mean can you blame her? …

SAL	So she has a go at Robyn, but Marcus sticks up for her – and, well …
KATIE	… You know Sarah Hartley.
SAL	She totally went off on one.
RICKY	I wish she'd go off on one with me …
SAL/KATIE	Shut up Ricky!
KATIE	So Sarah starts shouting …
SAL	Screaming more like …
KATIE	At Marcus …
SAL	… accusing him of all sorts of things.
LORNA	Like what?
SAL	Oh, you should have been there. She goes …
SARAH	Do you think I haven't seen you flirting before? *(To **Robyn**.)* Don't think you're so special, he's flirted with every girl in the school. *(To **Marcus**.)* If I wasn't so understanding I'd have dumped you last week when I saw you chatting up Amy Jones.
SAL	And so Marcus gets all angry and …
KATIE	No, no. First Robyn says …
ROBYN	He wasn't flirting with me – we were just talking about my painting.
SARAH	Oh is that right?
MARCUS	Yeah it is. And I wasn't chatting up Amy Jones, either! You're just being stupid.
SAL	As you can imagine, this was not a good thing to say.
SARAH	Me, stupid? Is that what you want me to be, stupid? Here, you like her little painting. *(She grabs a brush and ruins the picture.)* What do you think of it now, eh?
LORNA	She didn't?
KATIE	Wait, wait, that's not all.

MARCUS Sarah what the hell are you doing?

ROBYN You bitch! That was for my portfolio. *(She grabs a brush and daubs **Sarah**.)*

LORNA Oh my God …

SAL I know! And then …

SARAH Marcus, are you just going to let her get away with that!?

SAL And Marcus just stands there.

Marcus folds his arms and makes no attempt to intervene.

SARAH That's it you thoughtless bastard. I never want to see you again.

RICKY So what did Marcus say?

MARCUS Fine.

LORNA/RICKY Fine!?

KATIE Yeah, calm as you like.

SAL So then Sarah loses it big time …

SARAH Ooooohaaargh! *(She throws a jar of water/paint at him then goes for **Robyn** with the brush. A melee ensues.)*

KATIE But then right, this guy walks in. This new guy. You've gotta see him. Way fit. And he just strolls in like we're not there.

SAL Then he walks over to Mr Cartwright's desk and just starts looking through the register.

KATIE Then he turns and looks around the room, and walks out again. Never said a word to anyone. It was really odd.

RICKY Then what?

KATIE Everyone just stares after him. One of those moments when it's like, what just happened?

SAL   Then Sarah stormed off and everything was normal.
Except that this new guy is all that anyone can talk
about.

KATIE   That's probably 'cause he's so fit.

*As they finish telling the story, three children emerge
from the group. They are **Lucy**, **Connor** and **Baz**, the
bullies. They are clearly scheming something and go over
to **Lorna** and friends intent on causing trouble.*

RICKY   So this was just a cute guy story? If you'd said at the
start I could have disappeared.

KATIE   And made all our dreams come true.

RICKY   Listen Katie ...

*Lucy throws a sweet wrapper at **Lorna**.*

KATIE   Hey! What did you do that for?

LORNA   *(To **Katie**.)* Don't.

LUCY   What – oh, sorry, are you talking to me? Do what?

KATIE   I saw you throw that Lucy.

LUCY   I don't know what you're talking about, but then you
lot always were a bit weird, right Baz?

BAZ   Yeah, bloody weird.

LORNA   Just go away.

LUCY   And you're the weirdest of them all, Moon.

CONNOR   A bit of a loony.

LUCY   Yeah Loony Moony, I like that.

*They laugh. **Baz** continues to laugh loudly when the
others stop.*

CONNOR   It's not that funny Baz.

BAZ   Right.

LUCY   Is that what they called you at your last school Loony
Moony?

CONNOR Have you always been this screwed up?

RICKY Leave her alone.

LUCY I'm sorry, pintsize, are you trying to be hard?

RICKY No, I just meant …

CONNOR No, you weren't trying to be hard, were you Ricky boy? In fact I don't think you said anything at all, did you?

Ricky shakes his head frantically.

CONNOR I thought not. Must have been the wind. Now pick that crap up, we don't want to see any littering, do we?

Ricky goes and picks it up.

SAL Don't be so horrible Connor.

LUCY Yeah Connor, you nasty, nasty boy you. You'll make him cry.

The school bell rings to bring an end to break.

LORNA Just leave us alone.

LUCY Sorry, Loony Moony, are we upsetting you? Are you going to burst into tears and run away again like when Daddy left?

LORNA Stop it …

CONNOR Is that what made you so weird, Loony Moony, do you come from a broken home?

KATIE Shut up. Leave her alone.

LUCY Or what?

KATIE Or else.

SAL Why can't you lot just sod off?

LUCY Oh, the inseparable dork sisters are going to give us hassle now, are they? Got to stick up for your Loony mate?

KATIE Listen you …

LUCY   Yeah, you startin'?

*A teacher wonders over. She is **Miss French**.*

MISS FRENCH   We aren't trying to cause trouble here are we Lucy? You don't want me to have to call your parents again, do you?

LUCY   We were just talking, Miss French.

MISS FRENCH   Well break is over. I think it's time you went to class.

LUCY   You and I are gonna fall out big time Katie.

***Bullies** exit.*

KATIE   Any time Lucy.

MISS FRENCH   Lorna, can I have a quick word?

***Lorna** stays with behind as the others move off and wait for her.*

MISS FRENCH   How are you feeling?

LORNA   Fine, Miss.

MISS FRENCH   Really? Mr Cook said that you almost fainted again in maths this morning.

LORNA   I think I'm allergic to sums, Miss, maybe I should be excused maths from now on?

MISS FRENCH   And you missed art altogether. Lorna, I know you don't want to talk about this, but you've been off sick countless times, and your grades are suffering.

LORNA   Sorry.

MISS FRENCH   I'm not telling you off Lorna. But you know where I am if you want to talk.

LORNA   Thanks.

MISS FRENCH   OK, now you'd better get to class. Just say it was my fault you're late.

***Miss French** exits. **Lorna** rejoins her friends.*

KATIE   So what did she want?

LORNA   Oh, nothing.

SAL   Don't let Lucy scare you Lorn. It's just because you're new. She always picks on the new kids.

RICKY   She picked on me when I started.

KATIE   *(Jokingly.)* Funny, we never minded that so much.

RICKY   Listen Katie …

LORNA   So what's with this new guy then?

They begin to move off to class.

SAL   We don't know. We've asked around, but no one knows anything.

KATIE   Yeah, it's weird. No one even knows where he's from.

Exit.

SCENE THREE LORNA'S HOUSE

Lorna's Mum is in the kitchen as Lorna comes downstairs.

MUM   Lorna, your dinner's ready.

LORNA   I'm not hungry. I didn't ask for anything did I?

MUM   Don't start talking back to me. I won't stand for it.

LORNA   Well stop hassling me then, I'm not hungry.

MUM   I won't have this rudeness Lorna, it's been hard enough without it.

Lorna's little brother Jamie, comes downstairs but before entering hears another argument and hides.

LORNA   Me! Its not me that's caused all the trouble round here, it's you and Dad!

MUM   Lorna – I know it's been hard on you and Jamie, but …

LORNA   But what? If you know how hard it's been then why didn't you just stay together?

19

MUM We've had this discussion – your Dad and I ...

LORNA Oh yes, what was it? 'We just don't love each other any more'. Just don't love me and Jamie enough to try and stay together more like – together like a normal family.

MUM Normal! Lorna, you don't know what you're talking about.

LORNA Stop treating me like a baby!

MUM Then stop acting like one! And sit down and eat your dinner.

Lorna turns to go.

LORNA I said I'm not hungry.

MUM Lorna! *(Quietly.)* Lorna, please.

Jamie comes out of hiding and enters the kitchen, obviously concerned.

JAMIE Mum ...?

MUM Not now sweetheart, Mum's got a headache.

Jamie exits. Lights.

SCENE FOUR LORNA'S ROOM

Lorna is alone in her room, clearly agitated.

LORNA Why am I always the one in trouble?

She moves over to the mirror and touches it as though it holds some great secret.

SHADOW 1 She doesn't understand.

LORNA It's not like I broke up the family. It's their bloody fault. It wasn't me. I didn't do it. But I bet I didn't help.

*She begins to cry, but stops herself. Meanwhile her **Dad**, **Mum** and **Jamie** all emerge and she melts into a flashback of her **Dad** leaving.*

SHADOW 2 It makes no sense.

LORNA Dad, please don't leave. It's not right.

DAD I have to go, you know I do. But it's for the best.

LORNA How can it be for the best? You can't go! Stay, everything will get better. I'll be a better daughter, I promise. Mum … Mum make him stay? I'll be good.

SHADOW 3 She can't cope.

DAD Lorna, it's not about you. I'll still see you and Jamie. You can come and stay some weekends. Now come on, give me a hug eh?

He hugs them both.

LORNA Please Dad, don't go.

DAD I'll see you both in a couple of days. It's going to be fine.

LORNA Well you won't see me!

She runs off.

SHADOW 4 She doesn't know what's coming.

MUM Lorna …

DAD Sue, should I …

MUM Just go Paul. I'll see to it.

*She follows **Lorna**.*

JAMIE Can I still come and see you, even if Lorna doesn't want to?

DAD Of course you can, but give me a couple of weeks to get settled first. You'll look after your sister for me won't you?

JAMIE Yes, Dad. Bye.

DAD Bye, son.

SHADOW 5 It's time.

> *Jamie exits and **Lorna** re-enters to watch her **Dad** waving goodbye. Then he is gone.*

LORNA Nice one Lorna, get yourself all upset. And if you keep talking to yourself like this everyone's going to think you're mental.

> *Suddenly the **Girl** appears behind her. She is unaware of it, but then seems to sense something. **Jamie** breaks the tension, the **Girl** disappears.*

JAMIE Lorna, it's Jamie. Are you OK?

> *There is no answer.*

JAMIE Can I come in?

LORNA No.

JAMIE Why not?

LORNA What do you want?

JAMIE To come in would be nice.

> ***Lorna** softens.*

LORNA Alright you little troublemaker, come in.

JAMIE Thank you, your majesty.

LORNA Don't get cheeky or I'll send you out again.

JAMIE No you won't.

LORNA And why not?

JAMIE Because I'm great and you love me.

LORNA Oh is that why?

> *She grabs him and starts tickling him.*

JAMIE Get off – aahhh – Lorn I mean it, I'll use karate!

LORNA Go on then, Bruce Lee, make your move.

JAMIE I can't if you keep tickling me!

> *She stops and lets him go.*

LORNA   Anyway, you don't know karate.

JAMIE   Do so.

LORNA   Oh yeah, how?

JAMIE   I've seen it on TV – and I read some stuff on the Net.

LORNA   Well, you must be a black belt then.

JAMIE   Too right.

He starts doing mock karate movements.

JAMIE   You going to that party tonight?

LORNA   No.

JAMIE   Why not?

LORNA   What's the point?

JAMIE   The point is that everyone else will go and have fun and you'll be sat in your room sulking.

LORNA   I am not sulking.

JAMIE   Yes you are. You should go. You might meet this new guy everyone's talking about.

LORNA   I haven't got anything to wear.

Her mobile phone begins to ring. She goes to answer it.

JAMIE   Why do girls always say that? You've got loads more clothes than me, and I never moan about it. 'Ooh I've got nothing to wear, whatever will I do?'

Sal and Katie are on the phone, getting ready for the dance.

LORNA   Hello.

SAL   Hey Lorn it's Sal. You coming tonight?

LORNA   What is this, a conspiracy?

SAL   What?

LORNA   Nothing, look, I don't feel like a party tonight.

SAL You don't feel like anything lately. And Ricky said you chucked your lunch away again. Have you eaten anything today?

LORNA Yes, I've just had my dinner. You sound like my Mum, Sal.

SAL I'm just worried about you. You've been a bit down lately.

LORNA Gee, I wonder why that is?

SAL Don't be stupid, you know what I mean. Anyway, we reckon you could do with a night out, don't we Katie?

Katie takes the phone.

KATIE Come on hon, it'll do you good. Plus that new guy might be there, and he's dead fit. My Dad's giving us a lift, we'll swing by and pick you up in an hour. See ya soon. Bye.

LORNA Wait Katie ... Oh crap.

JAMIE What's up?

LORNA Come on you stirrer, get out, I've got to get ready, I've only got an hour.

JAMIE You going to the party?

LORNA No, that was NASA. One of their astronauts has 'flu and they need a replacement. I'm off to the moon in an hour.

Jamie looks puzzled – he is thinking this over.

LORNA Of course I'm going to the party, now get out, I have to change.

He goes to leave.

LORNA Oi, come here you.

They hug.

LORNA Thanks kiddo.

JAMIE Love you.

Lorna	Love you too.

He goes to leave again.

Lorna	Jamie?
Jamie	Yeah?
Lorna	D'you remember when we moved here, old Mr Barness told us that a girl had died in this house?
Jamie	Sort of. What about it?
Lorna	It's just … well, have you noticed anything funny around here recently?
Jamie	Is this a trick question?
Lorna	Not with Mum and Dad, I mean … anything weird, like … like a feeling. I was in here yesterday and I could have sworn …
Jamie	What?
Lorna	Oh nothing. It doesn't matter.
Jamie	OK. Have fun tonight.
Lorna	*(Distracted.)* Yeah … thanks.

***Jamie** leaves. **Lorna** begins getting ready.*

Scene Five The Kitchen

*Jamie enters the kitchen to talk to his **Mum**. She is washing up.*

Jamie	You alright, Mum?
Mum	Yes thank you sweetheart. Sorry, what was it you wanted earlier?
Jamie	Are you angry?
Mum	Who with?
Jamie	Lorna.

MUM   Your sister's having a hard time with your Dad gone. It's hard on us all.

JAMIE   It doesn't mean we won't see him anymore though does it?

MUM   No, of course not.

JAMIE   Well, I'm at school all day and I never see him then anyway. Will he still come and watch me play football?

MUM   Yes, I'm sure he will.

JAMIE   Will you?

MUM   Of course – when I can.

JAMIE   Then it will be alright, won't it?

MUM   I think I should have got you to talk to Lorna about all this, you know. You're much better at it than I am.

JAMIE   What, really?

MUM   Yes.

JAMIE   Is that good?

MUM   Yes, darling.

JAMIE   Can I have a new bike?

MUM   No.

JAMIE   Aww.

Exit.

SCENE SIX LORNA'S ROOM – THE VOICE

Lorna is in front of a full-length mirror half-heartedly inspecting her outfit/hair. She seems preoccupied with the mirror, touching it with reverence, almost fearful. (This scene may be underscored with music which rises steadily as the tension increases.)

VOICE   *(In surround sound/unfocused)* Lorna. Lorna.

LORNA   Jamie is that you?

Voice Lorna.

Lorna Cut it out Jamie. Do you hear me?

Voice Do you hear me?

Lorna Jamie? Mum? Who's there?

Voice Who is not there?

Lorna Alright, who is that?

Voice I've come for you. It is your turn now.

Lorna Stop it, stop it!

Voice Come with me.

Lorna Please ...

She covers her ears.

Voice Lorna.

Lorna *(Screams.)* No!

There is the sound of a doorbell – the underscoring cuts abruptly and the voice is gone.

Jamie *(Offstage.)* Lorna, Katie's here!

Lorna I'm just coming.

Exit.

Scene Seven The Party

Loud music, one at a time people run onto stage and assume position, then as one they begin to dance etc ...

Ricky is sat alone looking miserable, watching a girl try and persuade the new boy to dance. He obviously refuses. Lorna, Sal and Katie enter, and Lorna pulls Sal to one side.

Lorna Sal, I've got to tell you something.

Sal What is it?

Lorna I don't really know. Something happened to me at the house.

SAL What do you mean, something bad? Something serious?

LORNA Yes … well no, I think so – look I'm not really sure.

SAL Come on Lorn, what's wrong?

LORNA I heard a voice. It was calling me.

SAL Who was calling you?

LORNA The voice.

SAL Whose voice?

LORNA I don't know, it was just a voice.

SAL I'm starting to really worry about you Lorna. You're hardly eating, which is bad enough. And now you're hearing voices.

LORNA Not voices, a voice.

SAL It was probably just Jamie.

LORNA It wasn't Jamie.

SAL Come on Lorn, I'm sure it was nothing. Anyway, a good dance'll cheer you up.

LORNA I'm not in the mood.

Ricky and Katie come over to them.

RICKY Hey guys, where have you been? I've been bored stiff.

KATIE What, no one to dance with – big surprise there then.

RICKY Yeah, well I don't see anyone queuing up to dance with you either. But I'll tell you what, you know that new guy – I think he's called Craig – he's proving very popular.

He gestures to where the new boy is stood.

He's kind of mysterious. Maybe I should try that.

SAL It'll take more than a bit of mystery for you to get a date. Anyway, I heard his name was Carl.

RICKY   It's Craig – I mean, who's called Carl?

KATIE   Listen to you two. I can almost hear the wedding bells.

SAL   Now that's not funny, Katie.

RICKY   Yeah, I'm way out of her league.

KATIE   You're a bit quiet Lorn. Are you feeling alright?

She nods.

KATIE   Looks like Sarah Hartley got over Marcus pretty quickly.

They watch as she flirts with the new guy. Her advances are spurned.

RICKY   Oh my God – he totally blew her off! Is he crazy?

SAL   I'm sure he knows what he's doing.

LORNA   Hey, he's coming this way.

*They all turn to face him as he approaches. He goes straight up to **Lorna**.*

NEW GUY   Hi, I'm Chris.

RICKY/SAL   Chris?!

***Chris** turns towards them in surprise.*

CHRIS   Do I know you?

SAL   No, er …

KATIE   We were just leaving.

SAL   Yeah, that's right.

***Sal** and **Katie** go to leave but **Ricky** stays.*

RICKY   Are you sure your name isn't Craig?

***Sal** and **Katie** grab **Ricky**.*

SAL   See ya later Lorn.

RICKY   Good luck Lorn!

They muffle him and pull him away.

CHRIS   Well they're … interesting.

LORNA   What do you want? I'm sorry, I mean, why are you here?

CHRIS   Where?

LORNA   Here, now, talking to me.

CHRIS   Do you want me to go away?

LORNA   No, I mean, well not no, if you want to …

CHRIS   You're Lorna right, Lorna Moon?

LORNA   That's right. And you are Chris. Chris …?

CHRIS   Just Chris.

LORNA   So how did you know my name, just Chris?

CHRIS   I asked someone. Look, I was just leaving. This er … well, I really don't like this music. But I just wanted to come over and say hello first. It was nice to meet you, Lorna Moon, I'll see you around.

LORNA   Bye, just Chris.

He leaves and the gang return.

SAL   So what happened – why did he leave?

LORNA   I don't know. I think he has something against the music.

KATIE   So where's he from?

LORNA   I don't know.

SAL   What's he like?

LORNA   I don't know.

RICKY   These mysterious types, you can't trust 'em.

LORNA   Look, I'm going to get something to drink.

Lights/Music fade.

SCENE EIGHT THE GHOST

Lorna enters.

LORNA   Well that was an interesting evening.

VOICE   Lorna.

LORNA   Jesus. Who's there?

There is a crash of thunder and the lights go out. A power cut.

LORNA   A power cut, it's just a power cut.

VOICE   Come with me.

LORNA   No. No, this is all in my head.

VOICE   Come with me, Lorna.

LORNA   Stop it. Who are you?

VOICE   I have come for you.

LORNA   This is not happening.

VOICE   Come with me. It is the only way.

LORNA   Whoever you are, just go away! Please! Please just leave me alone!

VOICE   It's too close. Come with me … you must …

*The **Girl** appears through **Lorna's** mirror.*

Lorna.

*Lorna screams and runs out of her room. Her **Mum** appears, worried.*

MUM   Lorna. What is it, what's wrong?

LORNA   In the mirror – I saw something.

MUM   You saw what? Lorna, what happened?

LORNA   The – the light went out, and then I saw someone. A person.

MUM   Your lights did wha … What do you mean you saw someone? Where?

LORNA   In the mirror.

MUM   Lorna …

LORNA   Really, I saw someone – a girl.

MUM   For God's sake, I thought we had a burglar. What on earth are you thinking, screaming like that?

LORNA   But Mum …

The telephone begins to ring.

MUM   Lorna, you've got to stop all this nonsense now. Do you want people to think you're mental?

*She leaves. **Lorna** hesitantly examines the mirror and then sits down in the corner, terrified. Her **Mum** answers the phone.*

MUM   Hello.

DAD   Sue, it's Paul. Did you get my message about the CDs I left?

MUM   Yes. Paul …?

DAD   What is it?

MUM   Lorna's acting very strangely. I think we might have to get her some help.

DAD   Help? What, like a psychiatrist? It isn't like Lorna being odd is a new phenomenon, you know.

MUM   Look, you don't understand. She's been getting worse ever since the divorce.

DAD   I don't see how that's my fault.

MUM   What are you talking about? I never said it was.

DAD   Look, don't get all angry. If you could put those CDs in the post that would be great.

MUM   You can get them when you see the kids this weekend.

DAD   Oh, about that. I'm kind of busy this weekend, so it might be pushing it a bit to try and fit them in.

MUM   Fit them in? They're your children!

DAD   Don't get excited! God, you always do this, it isn't like I'm abandoning them. I've got a life to lead as well you know.

MUM   Fine, then you tell them.

DAD   What would that achieve? Look, could you just post me the CDs?

She hangs up the phone. Lights. Music.

SCENE NINE PARANOIA AT SCHOOL

Lorna stands centre stage and is surrounded by the Shadow Chorus who move around her threateningly. She seems to sense something of their presence, like a sense of foreboding. They are whispering 'Loony Moony's hearing voices'.

LORNA   Look, I just won't tell anybody – as long as they don't find out, I'll be OK. No one will know I'm losing my bloody mind.

Children now filter onto the stage behind her. The Shadow Chorus whisper to the children who also begin to whisper 'Loony Moony's hearing voices'. The volume rises steadily and the children move forwards threateningly. Lorna is terrified and as their chant reaches a crescendo she screams and falls to the floor. The school bell sounds loudly and the lights revert to 'normal' – the atmosphere is broken. There is silence and instantly the children are in school, looking at Lorna strangely.

KATIE   Are you alright, Lorn?

LORNA   Yeah, I'm fine.

KATIE   *(Suggestively.)* Any sign of Chris today?

LORNA	No. Why?
KATIE	Just wondering.

Ricky comes over.

RICKY	Hey guys, did you do the homework?
KATIE	What homework?
RICKY	I'm going to go out on a limb and say you haven't done it.
LORNA	Have you done it then Ricky?
RICKY	Sort of.
KATIE	Ooh, let's have a guess ...
KATIE/LORNA	You copied Robyn's.
KATIE	You always copy her. What will you do when she isn't in your class?
RICKY	I'll fail.

Sal comes over.

SAL	Hi guys. How are you feeling, Lorn?
RICKY	Why, what's wrong?
LORNA	Nothing. *(Stares meaningfully at **Sal**.)* Nothing's wrong.

*Mdm Blanc enters. **Lorna** pulls **Sal** aside and whispers urgently to her.*

LORNA	Sal, I have to talk to you later. Something else happened.
SAL	What do you mean?
LORNA	You know the voice I told you about? Well I saw someone ...
SAL	What?
LORNA	In my room last night, a girl ...
SAL	There was a girl in your room?

LORNA I don't know.

She is cut off as class begins.

MDM BLANC Bonjour la classe.

ALL Bonjour madame.

MDM BLANC J'espère que tout le monde s'est bien amusée hier soir a la boum?

The class look blank.

MDM BLANC I said class, I hope everyone had fun at the party last night.

SARAH We didn't all have fun Mademoiselle Blanc.

MARCUS Yeah, some of us couldn't get a dance Miss.

Laughter.

MDM BLANC Silence, Marcus. Continue please Sarah, why didn't you enjoy yourself, en Française, s'il vous plait?

SARAH Because Marcus is un grand tosser!

Laughter.

MDM BLANC Really Sarah, I expect more of you! That sort of language has no place in my classroom. Besides which, tosser is not a French word.

MARCUS Mademoiselle Blanc, I was just wondering, what is the French for bitch?

Laughter.

MDM BLANC Tais toi Marcus! Vous n'allez pas amener vos disputes ridicules dans ma classe et vous comporter comme des bebes!

They all look blank.

MARCUS Sorry Miss?

MDM BLANC I said shut up. Now, I believe we were looking at verbs. Lucy, veux tu commencer la leçon en conjugant le verbe etre?

Lucy   What Mademoiselle Blanc?

Mdm Blanc   I asked if you would start us off by declining the verb etre, to be.

Lucy   That's what I thought you said Miss. I'm better at French than you give me credit for you know.

Mdm Blanc   Is that right? Comment t'appelle tu?

Lucy   Oui Madame, je suis un chien.

Laughter.

Mdm Blanc   Lucy, what did I just ask you?

Lucy   If I had any pets Miss.

Mdm Blanc   I'm afraid Lucy I asked you your name, to which you replied, 'Yes Miss, I am a dog'.

More laughter.

Ricky   Well at least she wasn't lying Miss!

*Lucy stands and looks pointedly at **Lorna**. Meanwhile **Sal** is trying to pass a note to **Katie**.*

Lucy   I might be crap at French but at least I'm not totally mental.

Mdm Blanc   Silence! Now … Sally Jenkins, qu'est que tu as donc la?

Sal   What Miss?

Mdm Blanc   *(She sighs, exasperated.)* I said, what is that you have there?

Sal   What? Where Miss?

Mdm Blanc   Do you think I am stupid, Sally? Donne moi ca.

Sal looks for help then shrugs.

What, have you learned nothing, do any of you speak a word of French?

Ricky   Oui Mademoiselle!

Laughter.

MDM BLANC   Tais toi Ricky! Silence tout le monde.

*In the meantime **Sal** tries to pass the note to **Katie**. **Lucy** grabs the note off her.*

LUCY   Mademoiselle Blanc, I've got it, it's a note Miss. 'Katie, you know how I said she is hearing voices. Now she says she is seeing things ...' Ooh, I wonder who they're talking about?

BAZ   Ha, ha. Lorna's lost it. Lorna the Loon!

CONNOR   Yeah, Loony Moony's hearing voices!

*Laughter. **Lorna** stands and grabs her bag.*

LORNA   Thanks a lot Sal.

She runs out of the class.

SAL   Lorna wait.

MDM BLANC   Lorna! Where is that strange girl going now? Silence. Asseyez-vous Sally, I think you've caused enough trouble.

SAL   Me? She read the note out.

MDM BLANC   Now, Ricky, please decline the verb 'etre', 'to be'.

RICKY   Aren't you going to go after her Miss, see how she is?

MDM BLANC   I know how she is Ricky, she is upset. Etre, s'il vous plait.

RICKY   *(Continuing as scene changes.)* Je suis. Tu es. Il est. Elle est. Nous sommes. Vous êtes. Ils sont. Elles sont.

Lights.

SCENE TEN CHRIS & LORNA

***Lorna** is walking home in tears.*

CHRIS   Hi.

LORNA   Oh shit, don't do that. You nearly gave me a heart attack.

CHRIS   Sorry, I didn't mean to scare you. But hey, at least you've stopped crying.

LORNA   Yeah, thanks a million.

CHRIS Where are you going?

LORNA Anywhere but here.

CHRIS Fancy some company?

LORNA Look, shouldn't you be in class or something?

CHRIS Shouldn't you?

LORNA Fair play. But to be honest, I just want to be left alone.

CHRIS Nobody really wants to be left alone. Come on, let's go and get some lunch or something.

LORNA I'm not hungry. Look, you don't want to get to know me. Haven't you heard, I'm the loony who hears voices in her bedroom?

CHRIS Whose voice was it?

LORNA What?

CHRIS The voice you heard.

LORNA I don't know – look, it's all just too weird to talk about.

CHRIS You don't have to tell me if you don't want to.

LORNA Well, when we moved here, this old man who lives next door, Mr Barness, told us some girl had died in our house, or something like that.

CHRIS So?

LORNA Well – no, you'll think I'm crazy too.

CHRIS Try me.

LORNA I think I saw her.

CHRIS But she's dead.

LORNA I know that.

CHRIS A ghost?

LORNA I don't believe in ghosts.

CHRIS Well what else would you call her? Unless you think you imagined the whole thing.

LORNA Maybe I did, but I hope I never see her again.

CHRIS What if you do?

LORNA I'll probably get committed. Ow!

She doubles up in pain.

CHRIS What is it? Lorna?

LORNA It's just a stomach ache. I'll be OK in a minute.

CHRIS That seems like a pretty sudden stomach ache. Are you gonna be alright?

LORNA They never last long.

CHRIS You sure? Look, maybe you should sit down for a second, huh? *(He helps her.)* So what's with those kids who pick on you?

LORNA What? Oh, you mean Lucy and Connor and that lot. They pick on everyone. Guess I'm just flavour of the month 'cause I'm going mental.

CHRIS Don't say things like that. You're not going mental.

LORNA Seeing ghosts, hearing voices? I mean, you don't believe me, do you?

CHRIS Have you tried telling your family?

LORNA It's not the most supportive of environments back home right now. My little brother's cool though.

CHRIS You've told him?

LORNA Not exactly.

CHRIS Well he can't be all that cool then.

LORNA Hey …

CHRIS Well it just sounds like if he was any use you'd have told him about all this. And anyway, he should know something's up if he really cares, right?

LORNA Look you don't understand, it's been weird at home for a while.

CHRIS   So? I mean, I don't mean to sound rude, but it sounds to me like no one really cares enough to help you out.

LORNA   *(Sarcastically.)* But you do?

CHRIS   Maybe if you show a bit more belief in yourself people will be more responsive. For starters, why listen to those guys when they call you mental ...

LORNA   I think the correct term is 'Loony Moony'.

CHRIS   See, you're laughing about it now. Maybe that's the best response. Ignore it, just laugh it off.

LORNA   That's easier said than done ... and anyway, what do you know, I bet no one ever picks on you.

CHRIS   You don't know that, bullying could be the bane of my life.

LORNA   *(She shoves him playfully and they laugh together.)* Yeah right, and my biggest problem is turning down roles in smash hit movies!

CHRIS   Come on, I'll walk you home.

Then there is one of those awkward silences that acknowledge two people might be getting closer.

CHRIS   So is that what you'd like to do, become an actress?

LORNA   I don't know. I guess. I used to really enjoy drama and stuff, but lately ...

CHRIS   Lately what?

LORNA   Lately – well I just haven't been into stuff like I used to be, y'know? Like that party, that's the first time I've been out in god knows how long. I've become like a recluse, this weird hermit who surfaces to go to school and then disappears without trace back to her cave.

CHRIS   Well you don't look like a weird old hermit to me.

LORNA   Thanks ... I think.

They exit.

SCENE ELEVEN JAMIE & MR BARNESS

Jamie appears, not looking where he is going.

MR BARNESS	Hello Jamie.
JAMIE	Oh hi Mr Barness.
MR BARNESS	How's your Mum, I haven't seen her for a while?
JAMIE	She's alright. Getting used to stuff.
MR BARNESS	How's your sister?
JAMIE	She's OK I guess. Mr. Barness, can I ask you something?
MR BARNESS	Alright Jamie.
JAMIE	Well, it's just … it's about what you told us … erm … when we moved here.
MR BARNESS	You want to know about the dead girl don't you?
JAMIE	How did … how did you know that?
MR BARNESS	I knew you'd ask more about that some day. Everyone who lives in that house does.
JAMIE	So who was she?
MR BARNESS	Her name was Emily Parfitt.
JAMIE	What happened to her?
MR BARNESS	Emily was a nice girl, smiley you know. Then people noticed her acting – well acting strangely I suppose, all of a sudden. She rarely left her room. Seemed scared of her own shadow when she did. Her parents despaired of her. She seemed very depressed.
JAMIE	Why?
MR BARNESS	No one really knows. Anyway, she seemed to be getting better, had herself a new boyfriend and all that, but then one day – out of nowhere – well, they found her in the river at the foot of your garden, there.
JAMIE	She drowned? When was this?

Mr Barness	Oh, about twenty years ago now. Anyway, I must be getting inside. Even a fit young man like myself can only be up so long before his favourite armchair starts to call him.
Jamie	Thanks Mr Barness.
Mr Barness	That's alright. Say hello to your sister for me.
Jamie	I will.
Mr Barness	Jamie ... what made you ask about this?
Jamie	Oh, no reason. Bye.
	Exit.

Scene Twelve Walking Home

Chris and *Lorna* are walking home.

Lorna	... so now Dad lives in an apartment in town and I'm stuck at home until I'm old enough to move out.
Chris	Don't you like it at home?
Lorna	Not really, not anymore.
Chris	Why?
Lorna	Do you always have to ask so many questions? Why don't you tell me something about you?
Chris	Like what?
Lorna	Like anything, I don't even know your surname.
Chris	I suppose not.
Lorna	Well what is it?
Chris	*(Avoiding the question.)* So where exactly do you live?
Lorna	Just round the corner. But you never answered my question. Don't you have any problems? You know all about mine. Bet your problems are stuff like 'hmm, which girl should I take out tonight? I'd better consult my little black book'.

CHRIS Cut it out, why would a girl look twice at me?

LORNA Every girl in school has looked twice at you.

CHRIS Including you?

LORNA I, er … I mean I … I have to get home.

CHRIS Look, my biggest problem has always been the same. My er … sister.

LORNA Your sister?

CHRIS Yeah. Christ she's such a nightmare. She's one of those people who always has to win you know … er …

LORNA Ultra competitive?

CHRIS Well, you could say that yeah, although she takes it way further than that. I'm not sure she's all there to be honest.

LORNA So why's she like that, do you think?

CHRIS I don't really know. She's younger than me, and she always wanted to prove she was as good as her big brother, but she takes it way too far. I hate her, and I always have. And I know she hates me too. She's always looking to get one over on me – and she usually does.

LORNA She sounds fun. Can't wait to meet her.

CHRIS Trust me, you don't want to. Anyway, I have to go now. Can I meet you after school tomorrow?

LORNA Sure, if you want to.

CHRIS Great. I'll see you then.

LORNA See ya.

CHRIS Bye.

Lights.

43

SCENE THIRTEEN THE ARGUMENT

Lorna enters followed by *Jamie.*

LORNA   Hey Jamie.

JAMIE   Hiya. Who was that guy I saw you with?

LORNA   What guy?

JAMIE   Outside, I saw you walking home with him. Who was he?

LORNA   Just a friend from school.

JAMIE   What's his name.

LORNA   God you're such a nosy little git aren't you?

JAMIE   And his name is ...?

LORNA   Chris, his name's Chris.

JAMIE   Chris what?

LORNA   Right, that's it ...

Lorna goes to grab him and he starts doing his mock karate moves. She pins him down.

JAMIE   I should warn you, I'm trained to get out of any hold instantly.

LORNA   So why aren't you escaping this one then?

JAMIE   If you must know, I am currently assessing the situation.

LORNA   You little ... *(She starts tickling him again.)*

JAMIE   Alright ... stop, please, I give up!

Lorna lets him up.

JAMIE   Lorna, you know what you were talking about the other day?

LORNA   About how I never have anything to wear?

JAMIE   Yeah OK. No, about that girl, the one that died.

LORNA   Yeah, go on.

JAMIE I asked Mr Barness about it today.

LORNA Really? What did he say?

JAMIE He said that she drowned in the river, in our garden.

LORNA Jesus. Did he say what her name was?

JAMIE Emily something ... Parfitt, Emily Parfitt.

LORNA Jamie, you know how I've been acting a bit off recently ...?

JAMIE Has this got anything to do with what happened at school today?

LORNA What?

JAMIE Everyone's talking about it. Saying you've gone mad and stuff.

LORNA Oh great, that's just what I need. And I suppose you believe them?

JAMIE What? Of course I ...

LORNA Forget it Jamie.

JAMIE But Lorna ...

LORNA I said forget it, alright! Just piss off and leave me alone!

JAMIE What's got into you?

LORNA Just leave me alone. What help have you ever been?

JAMIE What? Lorna ...

Jamie exits, leaving *Lorna* alone.

SCENE FOURTEEN CLOSING IN

*We hear the voice of the **Girl**.*

GIRL Your pain has brought me to you Lorna. And now you must come with me. You don't understand yet, but you will.

Lorna and *Chris* enter.

LORNA Thanks for walking me home ... and the chat. I haven't really talked about this stuff before.

CHRIS That's OK. It was nice. I'll see you tomorrow?

LORNA Sure. Whose classes are you in?

CHRIS We'll run into each other at break.

LORNA OK. Bye, just Chris.

CHRIS See ya.

LORNA Chris?

CHRIS Yeah?

LORNA I ... oh it doesn't matter.

CHRIS No, go on, it's OK.

LORNA Why ... why did you ask me to dance when all those other girls wanted to dance with you?

CHRIS I didn't ask you to dance.

LORNA You know what I mean.

CHRIS I don't know – 'cause you look nice I guess.

LORNA You didn't like ... feel sorry for me.

CHRIS What?

LORNA It's just that I wouldn't want to think you were nice to me because ... well because I'm a charity case or something.

CHRIS Lorna, don't be silly. I'm nice to you because I like you. If I hadn't come over and talked with you that time I'd never have found out ... you know, how ... nice you are.

LORNA Really?

CHRIS Really.

> *Lorna* leans in as though to kiss *Chris* and he is taken off guard. He backs off hurriedly.

LORNA   Sorry I ... I thought ...

CHRIS   Lorna I ... *(Lorna runs away.)* Lorna wait. I'm sorry.

Chris forlornly turns and walks away, annoyed with himself. Lorna goes into her bedroom, agitated and confused. Jamie appears at the door.

JAMIE   Lorna. I'm sorry about yesterday ... but I didn't believe them, I promise.

LORNA   What are you talking about. Believe who?

JAMIE   The people at school, the ones who said you were going mad. I didn't believe them, really.

LORNA   *(Softens.)* I know you didn't ... you can come in you know.

Jamie enters. He bows graciously.

JAMIE   Once more at your service, your majesty.

LORNA   You've been watching too many 'Robin Hood' films.

JAMIE   It's a well-known fact that no boy can watch too many 'Robin Hood' films.

LORNA   God, sometimes you sound more grown up than Dad!

JAMIE   Really? Cool.

Jamie notices she seems upset.

JAMIE   What's wrong Lorn? You don't look very happy.

LORNA   It's just been a weird day.

JAMIE   Like how?

LORNA   It just has OK.

JAMIE   But like how has it ...

LORNA   Jamie ... look, I'm not in the mood for one of your question and answer sessions right now, alright?

JAMIE   I'm just worried about you ...

LORNA   Worried? Being nosy and being worried aren't the same thing you know. Asking me a thousand questions just to piss me off isn't being worried, it's being a stupid little child.

JAMIE   What are you talking about? You know that's ...

LORNA   Shut up! You don't care. Mum doesn't care. Just get out Jamie, I want to be alone.

Jamie, utterly crestfallen and confused, exits.

Lorna has sudden remorse and looks like she is going to go after him when the underscoring is heard and she senses the presence of the Girl.

LORNA   I know who you are! I know. You're Emily Parfitt aren't you? You drowned in the river! I know I'm right. Do you hear me? And I'm not afraid of you.

GIRL   Yes you are.

LORNA   Where are you?

GIRL   You're not playing by the rules. I need you Lorna. I need you here.

LORNA   Why can't you just leave me alone?

GIRL   If you won't come with me Lorna, then I'll come to you. *(With real malice.)* I'm coming Lorna.

Blackout, followed instantly by the sound of glass smashing.

LORNA   *(Screams.)* No!

End of Act One.

ACT TWO

SCENE ONE LORNA ALONE

Lorna is in her room, near the now broken mirror, alone and yet surrounded by the Shadow Chorus. There is a bandage on her arm. As she speaks the Shadow Chorus echo her thoughts, whispering 'Alone' and 'Not Alone' intermittently.

LORNA (*Softly.*) Alone. Alone, alone, alone. All I want is to be alone in my room again. That's how it used to be. If I was the only person here ... I was alone. On my own. Single, solitary, keeping my own company. Not any more though. Because you're here. Behind my mind, in my head. Behind the walls. (*She stoops to pick up a piece of broken mirror that was missed.*) In the mirror – or released from it! (*She makes as though to cut her other arm with the broken piece of mirror, then stops and begins to shout. The Shadows fall silent in that instant and begin to melt away.*) You're still here, aren't you? Only you're out now. But you haven't gone away have you? That would be far too easy. You won't leave me alone, so at least tell me why. You can't just spout a load of cryptic crap and leave me with it! I know you're there!

She falls to the ground crying.

Lights.

SCENE TWO DISCUSSING LORNA

Sal and Katie enter. They are talking about Lorna.

KATIE Has she spoken to you yet?

SAL No. I've called her like a hundred times but she won't return my calls.

KATIE Do you suppose she's still upset about the note?

SAL Wouldn't you be?

KATIE Did her mum tell you what happened to her?

SAL She thinks she slipped and fell into the mirror, that's how she cut herself. She lost some blood and that.

KATIE She wasn't in hospital long. Just a couple of days or so, I think. Do you believe her, about her arm?

SAL I don't know. It sounds a bit suss to me, and since it happened she's been locked in her room most of the time, so her mum says anyway.

KATIE Really? Weird.

SAL I keep trying to ring, but so far she won't talk.

Ricky walks over.

RICKY Hi guys.

SAL Hi Ricky.

RICKY Have you spoken to Lorna yet?

KATIE No. You?

RICKY I took round her French homework but she wouldn't see me. I mean, I can understand her being angry with you guys, but I didn't do anything.

KATIE Thanks Ricky, that's really thoughtful of you.

SAL He's right though.

RICKY Sal, what was it she told you, you know, about hearing stuff, or seeing something or whatever?

SAL She didn't really tell me anything. Besides, she's been so down recently, I think she was probably just … seeing things.

RICKY Didn't she tell you that?

SAL She told me she saw something, someone – a girl, she said she saw a girl. But what I mean is I don't think she really did see a girl – I think she's seeing things, hallucinating.

RICKY Why?

SAL   I'm not a bloody psychologist Ricky. I just reckon Lorna's been so upset that she's creating stuff like this in her head. She's confused, y'know?

KATIE   Hmm. You should be a shrink, you sound kinda like Sigmund Freud. You look a little like him from some angles.

Laughter. The school bell rings.

KATIE   Did we have any homework?

RICKY   Yeah, a couple of questions on *Hamlet*.

SAL   What, and you did it?

RICKY   Sort of. I copied Robyn's.

Exit.

SCENE THREE BACK IN LORNA'S ROOM

*The **Girl** appears and watches **Lorna**. **Jamie** appears at her door.*

JAMIE   Lorna, are you alright?

LORNA   What do you want?

JAMIE   Mum wants to know if you want some dinner.

LORNA   I'm not hungry.

JAMIE   Lorna, please eat something. Mum called the doctor today.

LORNA   Well what did he say then?

JAMIE   What did I do Lorna? Why are you being so horrible all the time?

LORNA   I said what did the doctor say?

JAMIE   I don't know, mum was talking to him, not me. Can't you just try and eat a little something?

LORNA   I told you I'm not hungry. I'm going to have a bath, tell mum I might get something later.

JAMIE   Yeah, sure. Look, can't I just come in for a minute?

LORNA   I want to be alone. *(Laughs strangely.)*

JAMIE   What's so funny?

LORNA   *(Still laughing.)* I want to be alone! Some bloody hope.

JAMIE   Are you OK Lorn?

LORNA   Oh just great. Tell you what Jamie, you make it so I can be alone in my own room and then I'll let you into my room. Pretty fair eh?

JAMIE   Are you sure you won't eat something?

LORNA   Yes, now go away. I'm going for a bath.

Jamie leaves.

Lorna is about to get undressed. The Girl speaks, but is still unseen by her.

GIRL   Lorna.

LORNA   Where are you?

GIRL   Behind you!

Lorna spins round but there is nothing there. The Girl laughs, coldly.

LORNA   Stop it! Leave me alone!

The Girl appears in the room.

GIRL   But I can't leave you Lorna. Then you would have no one.

LORNA   What? What do you ...

GIRL   No one cares about you. Your brother, your mother. I came when your father left. Your pain is what called to me. I cannot leave until it is over.

Chris appears and surprises them both. The Girl disappears.

CHRIS   Until what is over?

Lorna Jesus … what the are you doing here?

Chris I came round to see how you are. Are you talking to yourself?

Lorna How did you get in here.

Chris Jamie let me in. How are you feeling?

Lorna Better – I think.

Chris I've been worried about you.

Lorna You don't need to be, I'm OK.

Chris You don't look OK.

Lorna Wow, you really know how to flatter a girl, huh?

Chris That's not what I meant. You're beautiful and all, it's just that you look a little fragile, y'know?

Lorna You what?

Chris I said you look a little fragile …

Lorna Wait, wait … you said I was beautiful.

Chris Well yes but …

Lorna But what, you've changed your mind?

Chris No, look … Lorna, I didn't come here to … I mean …

Lorna What do you mean?

Chris I don't know. I just wanted to know you're OK, see if you needed a friend.

Lorna What, you mean like those nice people that made me look like a nutcase in front of the world?

Chris No, I mean a real friend.

*Lorna begins to sob and clings to **Chris**.*

Lorna Nobody cares about me Chris, nobody.

Chris I care Lorna. I promise.

*They kiss gently before **Chris** suddenly pulls away.*

CHRIS I'm sorry, I …

LORNA Look I'm trying to get ready for a bath anyway so … you should leave.

CHRIS Lorna I …

LORNA Just go Chris!

Chris turns and goes. Lorna cries.

SHADOW 1 I shouldn't have done that.

SHADOW 2 I know I need help.

SHADOW 3 What am I going to do now?

SHADOW 4 Where am I going to turn?

SHADOW 5 I'm all alone.

Lorna makes to go after Chris.

LORNA Chris wait …

Instead she comes face to face with the Girl. It backs up.

LORNA Talk. Say something! Please! You hurt me, at least tell me why!

GIRL It was necessary. It is your time now.

LORNA My time? What do you …?

GIRL He doesn't care about you either! No one cares. Come with me Lorna, it is the only way.

LORNA I don't know what you mean …

GIRL They were happy once. Without you. They can be happy again. Without you. They hate you because you drove them apart. Jamie hates you because you broke up his family.

LORNA No! Please, it's not true.

GIRL You know what you have to do. End your guilt Lorna, end your suffering, and end theirs …

The Girl backs out of the room and disappears.

Shadow 1	They were happy once.
Shadow 2	They would be happy now without you.
Shadow 3	They were happy without you.
Shadow 4	They don't love you.
Shadow 5	At least they could be a family for Jamie.
Shadow 1	Without you.
Lorna	No, it's not true. It's not all my fault.
Shadow 2	Your guilt is a terrible burden.
Shadow 3	You know what you have to do.
Girl	Come with me.

Lights.

Scene Four English Class

Miss French So for next week I would like you all to have read up to Act 2 Scene 3, OK?

The school bell rings.

Miss French See you all next week, have a nice weekend. Sally, Katie, can I see you for a moment please?

Sal Yes Miss?

Miss French I was just wondering if either of you know how Lorna is?

Katie Not really Miss …

Sal She's still recovering at home, not really ready for visitors.

Miss French I heard about what happened in Mademoiselle Blanc's class. Was she very upset?

Katie I think so, I mean she was at the time.

Sal The thing is Miss, she won't talk to me … to us … I mean, she hasn't spoken to us since that day.

KATIE	We've tried calling and all, but ...
MISS FRENCH	Alright girls, I understand. Look, try not to worry, she won't hold it against you forever.
KATIE	Thanks Miss French.

They turn to leave.

SAL	Oh Miss French, it might be worth asking Chris whether or not he's spoken to her.
MISS FRENCH	Who?
KATIE	Chris, that new kid. They seemed to be getting on quite well, but I haven't seen him around recently.
MISS FRENCH	I don't know of anyone joining the school recently. Are you sure this boy goes here?
SAL	Yes, I'm sure he does. I've seen him around school a couple of times.
MISS FRENCH	OK Sally, thank you.
SAL	Everything's alright, isn't it Miss?
MISS FRENCH	Oh, yes, I expect I just overlooked it, people come and go so often these days. You say his name is Chris, Chris what?
KATIE	I don't know Miss. Do you want me to find out?
MISS FRENCH	No, no, it's fine. Thanks for that girls, see you tomorrow.
SAL	Bye.

Sally and Katie exit. Miss French picks up a phone, then spies Mdm Blanc.

MISS FRENCH	Mademoiselle Blanc do you have a second?
MDM BLANC	Of course Joanne. What is it?
MISS FRENCH	Do you know anything about a new boy in school called Chris.
MDM BLANC	Chris what?

MISS FRENCH	I don't know. Just Chris.
MDM BLANC	I'm not very good with names.
MISS FRENCH	So no then?
MDM BLANC	No what?
MISS FRENCH	No you don't know of a new boy called Chris?
MDM BLANC	I just said that.
MISS FRENCH	OK, thank you anyway Michelle.

Mdm Blanc exits. **Miss French** *picks up the phone again and dials.*

MISS FRENCH Pauline, it's Joanne. Fine thanks, listen – do you know anything about a new intake? I don't know, a boy named Chris. No, Sally Jenkins told me about him, she doesn't know his surname. Thanks a lot Pauline. You'll let me know? Great, bye.

Lights.

SCENE FIVE RETURN OF THE PLAYGROUND MAFIA

The group of bullies are sat around talking.

BAZ … and then that guy like, kills himself 'cause it's all too much for him. *(Mimes killing himself.)*

CONNOR Yeah but what a wimp though. I would have gone to the police and turned myself in. They'd never have proved anything.

LUCY It was just a film guys, and I thought it was crap anyway. Besides, lots of people kill themselves. I would if I looked like you.

Katie and Sal walk near them.

CONNOR Reckon Loony Moony'll probably kill herself, don't you?

KATIE What did you say, Connor?

CONNOR What, what did I say?

KATIE	Don't try and be clever Connor, it doesn't suit you.
SAL	And don't talk about Lorna like that.
LUCY	He's right though, I mean, she must be way depressed after getting stabbed in the back by her two best mates.
CONNOR	And in front of the whole school.
SAL	Shut up you bastards!
LUCY	Just telling the truth.
BAZ	If you can't take it maybe you shouldn't be so horrible to her.
CONNOR	I mean, we make fun and all, but we never hurt no one.
LUCY	Never cause anyone serious psychological damage.

*They laugh. **Katie** suddenly lunges for **Lucy** and knocks her to the ground.*

KATIE	*(Almost in tears.)* It's not our fault you bitch! An' you'd better leave Lorna alone or else!
SAL	Come on Katie, let's go.
KATIE	She'll be alright won't she Sal? Lorna?
SAL	She'll be fine. Don't get upset.

*Sal and **Katie** exit. **Lucy** picks herself up and notices everyone is staring.*

LUCY	What?!

They exit.

SCENE SIX THE HAUNTING

*Lorna is in her room asleep, but standing up. The **Shadows** enter and begin to wrap her in a large sheet as she reacts as though in the midst of a nightmare.*

SHADOW 1	It hurts you now ...
SHADOW 2	It grows like a cancer ...
SHADOW 3	Consuming you with its intensity.

SHADOW 1   You sleep for fear of being awake …

SHADOW 2   But when you walk in the shadow of pain …

SHADOW 3   Of fear …

SHADOW 4   Of death …

SHADOW 5   Your fear knows no rest.

*The **Girl** emerges and walks across the stage. The **Shadows** unwrap **Lorna** from the sheet.*

SHADOW 4   Your dreams are the realm …

SHADOW 5   Of the world you cannot know.

SHADOW 1   And in the dark …

SHADOW 2   Treasure your memories …

SHADOW 3   Value them while you can.

GIRL   Remember that once you were loved Lorna Moon. Feel the loss now that you are despised. And you will come to me.

*The **Shadows** lay **Lorna** down and cover her with the sheet. **Lorna** is woken by her phone ringing. The **Girl** disappears.*

LORNA   Hello?

SAL   Lorna? Don't hang up, it's me, Sal.

LORNA   What do you want?

SAL   Don't be like that Lorna, you know I'm sorry. I just wanted to talk to you.

LORNA   What about?

SAL   Have you seen Chris recently?

LORNA   Why?

SAL   I'm just a bit worried. I mean, what do you know about him, Lorn?

LORNA   Nothing, really.

SAL   Do you know where he's from, or where he lives?

LORNA   No, I never asked him. What are you getting at?

SAL   Well, it's like ... have you noticed that you seem to have been acting ... well you know, you seem to have, been troubled I guess, ever since he turned up? I don't trust him.

LORNA   You don't know him!

SAL   Neither do you, you just said so.

LORNA   Look Sal, I don't need this right now, and you've no bloody right to ...

*Suddenly The **Girl** appears and **Lorna** breaks off distracted.*

SAL   Lorna, are you still there?

GIRL   Come with me Lorna. You know what you have to do.

SAL   Lorn – Lorna is that you, what's going on? Lorna, are you there?

GIRL   There is only one answer – come with me now.

SAL   What did you say? Only one answer? What are you talking about?

LORNA   I've got to go Sal. Goodbye.

SAL   Lorna wait!

***Lorna** turns off her phone.*

LORNA   I know who you are. I know what happened to you, Emily.

GIRL   No Lorna. Not Emily.

LORNA   What? But I thought ...

GIRL   Emily came with me Lorna. She is on the other side. You must come with me and end your pain.

LORNA   Emily went with you ...

***Lorna** seems hopelessly under the spell of the **Girl**.*

GIRL   You have no choice. Come with me Lorna.

Lorna goes towards the mirror. She looks at herself in the shattered fragments. When she turns round the Girl is gone again, but its voice is heard. Lorna's Mum is on the phone. A phone somewhere else is ringing. Her Dad answers.

DAD   Hello?

MUM   Hello Paul. It's Sue.

DAD   Hello.

GIRL   They were happy once, and they can be again. You know what you have to do. Come with me.

MUM   It's about Lorna. She still won't eat. I spoke to the doctor again.

SHADOW 1   *(Whispering.)* I know what I have to do.

SHADOW 2   I have seen the end.

DAD   Did you tell her how long this has been going on for?

SHADOW 3   They can be happy. I can find peace …

SHADOW 4   In the shadows.

MUM   Yes I told her. She said that minor eating disorders are common in teenage girls. She thinks it could be a result of her feelings about the divorce.

SHADOW 5   You know what you have to do.

LORNA   Oh I just want it to stop. *(She reverently touches the mirror.)* I know what I have to do.

Lights go down on Lorna who exits. The parents' phone conversation continues.

DAD   Listen if you want to start playing the blame game again I'll …

MUM   You'll what? What will you do Paul?

DAD   Just leave it Sue.

MUM	Listen Paul, just for once. The doctor said she'd probably come round on her own, and that we should try and talk to her. She said as long as there are no physical side effects we needn't worry too much, but to keep a close eye on her.
DAD	Good, that all sounds fair enough.
MUM	So when can you come round?
DAD	What?
MUM	If we're going to talk about the divorce, you should be here too.
DAD	Alright. I could probably do next week sometime ...
MUM	No Paul! For god's sake she's your daughter!
DAD	OK, OK. Tomorrow, is tomorrow evening alright?
MUM	Fine, I'll see you then.
	Lights.

SCENE SEVEN THE TURNING POINT

Sal, Katie and *Ricky* enter. *Ricky* is eating.

KATIE	God, you don't stop do you? One day you're gonna be so fat!
RICKY	Yeah, but I'll still be sexier than you.
KATIE	Ha, ha. Sal, I don't get why you're so down on Chris all of a sudden. Lorna was acting weird before he ever arrived.
SAL	She was just depressed because of the divorce. Things have got much worse recently. And don't you think it's weird how Miss French has never heard of him?
KATIE	Well he is new.
RICKY	What are you getting at Sal?
SAL	I don't know.

RICKY   Do you think he's up to something?

KATIE   Like trying to get close to Lorna?

RICKY   But why though?

SAL   Right – listen Dumb and Dumber, how about you two stop asking questions all the time and actually try thinking! I don't know why, I just think something's going on here, like he's playing with her head or something.

KATIE   Well, she has been getting worse.

RICKY   That doesn't mean it's his fault. You two were the ones who stitched her up in class.

KATIE   Will you stop going on about that!

SAL   Wait you guys. She said something strange to me on the phone the other night. She was being really weird. She sounded really distracted, like she was talking to someone else.

RICKY   Maybe she is going mad.

KATIE   Don't say that Ricky.

SAL   I'm worried guys. We need to find Chris, I'm sure he knows something about this, or else why all the mystery?

RICKY   So where do we look for him if he isn't around school?

Chris appears and walks over to them.

CHRIS   Hello. I need to talk to you. It's about Lorna.

SAL   Yeah, well we want to talk to you, Chris, or whatever your name is?

CHRIS   What's that supposed to mean?

KATIE   What have you done to Lorna?

CHRIS   Done to her? Look I …

SAL   She's been getting worse ever since you turned up out of nowhere.

CHRIS   Hang on a minute, let me get this straight. You're accusing me of causing all her problems when you were the ones who made her look so stupid in front of everyone.

KATIE   Hey that was an accident.

RICKY   Look, one way or another Lorna has been a different person and we think you know why.

KATIE   She certainly never heard voices or ... or hallucinated before you appeared.

SAL   That's right, and how come the teachers at school don't know who you are, eh?

CHRIS   Look, you don't understand ...

SAL   Explain it to us.

CHRIS   I can't.

KATIE   You can't or you won't?

CHRIS   Either way, I'm not telling you.

SAL   Then tell me this, when did you last see Lorna?

CHRIS   Yesterday.

SAL   And what did you say to her?

CHRIS   Not much. Why?

SAL   Because I spoke to her earlier today and she sounded really weird. Like she was talking to someone else. I swear she said 'come with me' – or at least, someone did.

CHRIS   What?

SAL   That's not the point, the point is ...

CHRIS   Listen! Tell me exactly what Lorna said to you.

SAL   Why?

CHRIS   Just tell me.

RICKY   Calm down Chris.

KATIE   What are you so stressed about?

CHRIS   Please, just tell me what she said.

SAL   I don't really know, like I said she was kind of distant ...

Chris turns and hurries away.

KATIE   Wait! Where's he going?

RICKY   Come on, let's go with him.

SAL   Yeah. I don't trust that guy.

All exit.

SCENE EIGHT PREPARING

Lorna is in her room, preparing as though going out for the evening. She is attended by the Shadows, who are mirroring her movements as she looks in the broken mirror.

SHADOW 1   I'm tired.

SHADOW 2   I look tired.

SHADOW 3   I want to rest.

SHADOW 4   Get some sleep.

SHADOW 5   I only want what's best ...

SHADOW 1   For everyone.

SHADOW 2   I'm all alone.

SHADOW 3   I don't want to be alone.

LORNA   I look strange today. Like a shadow ...

SHADOWS   ... or a ghost.

The Girl appears and beckons to her.

GIRL   It is time Lorna. Come with me.

The Girl exits.

LORNA   I don't recognise the face in the mirror anymore.

SHADOWS   It is time to go now.

*Lights fade as all follow the **Girl**.*

SCENE NINE RACE AGAINST TIME

Chris *arrives at **Lorna's** house closely followed by the others.*

RICKY   Wait up!

CHRIS   Why are you following me?

KATIE   We want to know what you're up to.

CHRIS   Well you can't so you might as well ...

SAL   No! I've had enough of your stupid secrets! Who do you think you are anyway, James Bond? Tell us what you know. Is Lorna in some sort of trouble?

Chris *hesitates.*

SAL   Tell us!

CHRIS   Alright. Alright. Look, I can't explain why, but I just have a really bad feeling about this. Something's wrong. I know it. You can take this seriously or leave, I don't have time.

*He turns and knocks on the front door. **Jamie** answers.*

JAMIE   Hello.

CHRIS   Is Lorna here?

JAMIE   She's upstairs. Hi Sal.

CHRIS   I need to see her.

JAMIE   I think she's probably asleep.

Chris *pushes past him.*

JAMIE   *(To **Sal**.)* Eager isn't he?

They find her room is empty.

JAMIE   Lorna! Where is she?

SAL   Where is she Chris, what's happening?

CHRIS   Oh no. The river.

SAL   Lorna!

*They all run off. The **Girl** appears and watches them go.*
Lights.

SCENE TEN THE RIVER

***Lorna** is walking towards the river. The **Shadows** are encouraging her.*

SHADOW 1   I've seen so much.

SHADOW 2   I want it to stop.

SHADOW 3   I need it to stop.

SHADOW 4   For Jamie, for Mum and Dad.

SHADOW 5   I need to rest

SHADOW 1   I know what I have to do.

*Suddenly **Lorna** gets one of her bouts of pain and falls to her knees. The **Girl** appears and beckons her.*

GIRL   Get up! You can't stop now. The pain will go forever if you finish it. But you must get up, Lorna. Come with me now!

SAL   *(Offstage, distant.)* Lorna!

LORNA   Sally?

GIRL   Voices of the past Lorna. Come with me.

SHADOW 1   He left and you cried.

SHADOW 2   Why did you cry?

SHADOW 3   For a father who doesn't love you?

SHADOW 4   For a mother who doesn't care?

SHADOW 5	For a brother who doesn't understand?
ALL SHADOWS	For yourself?

*Lorna gets up and continues into the river. She is drowning. The **Girl** fades into the background. The others, lead by **Chris**, come running on.*

CHRIS	Lorna!
JAMIE	Lorna! Oh no!

Lights.

SCENE ELEVEN IN HOSPITAL

*The **Shadow Chorus** are on stage, assembled as a group. All other characters appear and enclose the stage. **Lorna** is in the midst of them. The **Shadow Chorus** are constantly whispering the same lines over and over in a confused fashion.*

SHADOW 1	Where am I? I don't understand.
SHADOW 2	I don't want to talk to you. Just leave me alone.
SHADOW 3	You think I'm mad don't you?
SHADOW 4	But they pick on me, I can't go back.
SHADOW 5	It's all my fault, I know it is.
SHADOW 1	Why is this happening to me?
LORNA	I'm not talking to anyone! I'm OK now.
LUCY	Loony Moony's hearing voices.
MOTHER	We just don't love each other anymore.
BULLIES	Loony Moony's hearing voices.
DR LANE	Hello Lorna, my name is Dr Sheila Lane.

Shadow 1 exits.

LORNA	You'll think I'm crazy.
FATHER	I'm not moving far away …

DR LANE   It's alright Lorna, it's not at all unusual to hear certain things when you're upset. Don't worry, you're not crazy.

Shadow 2 exits.

ALL BULLIES   Loony Moony's hearing voices.

LORNA   But they were real.

MOTHER   Do you think the world revolves around you?

DR LANE   They tell me you haven't been eating very well. Do you want to tell me about it?

FATHER   I'll still see you, all the time.

LORNA   I didn't want to drive him away.

DR LANE   You didn't Lorna, you mustn't believe that.

Shadow 3 exits.

LORNA   Then why did he leave us?

ALL BULLIES   Loony Moony!

LORNA   What about the things I've seen?

DR LANE   It does happen Lorna. There are many reasons why this can happen …

Shadow 4 exits.

FATHER   Your Mum and I are separating from each other, not from you and Jamie.

DR LANE   So how do you feel today Lorna?

LUCY   Are you going to cry like when Daddy left?

LORNA   I feel a lot better actually Dr Lane.

DR LANE   I think it's about time you started calling me Sheila, don't you?

MOTHER   Lorna, I know it has been hard on you and Jamie.

Shadow 5 falls silent.

Dr Lane   So why don't you tell me more about your friend Chris.

Chris   I care Lorna. I promise.

Lorna   Did I imagine it all?

Shadow 5 exits. *The voices of* **Lorna** *and* **Dr Lane** *begin to fade out.*

Scene Twelve Mr Barness' News

Mr Barness is centre stage and is joined by Jamie.

Mr Barness   Ah, Jamie.

Jamie   Hello Mr Barness.

Mr Barness   I heard what happened to your sister, Jamie. I think there's something you ought to know.

Jamie   Like what?

Mr Barness   When you asked me about someone dying in your house. There's more to it than I told you. And now this has happened to your sister – you'd best come inside.

Exit.

Scene Thirteen Lorna Recovering

It is a few days later. **Lorna** *is in her room. There is a knock at the door.*

Lorna   Mum?

Chris   Not quite.

Lorna   Hey, how are you?

Chris   I'm OK. How are you?

Lorna   I'm doing fine. They only kept me in for observation, seems I've just got a bit of a chill. *(There is an awkward pause.)* Chris, I've been hoping you'd come by, I wanted to thank you. And also ...

*Chris kisses her suddenly. The lights fade on them but come up on **Mr Barness** and **Jamie**.*

MR BARNESS   I grew up in this town, Jamie. I've lived here all my life. What I told you about Emily Parfitt is true, but I didn't tell you that she wasn't the only person who died in your house.

JAMIE   What do you mean?

MR BARNESS   When I was little I was told a story about your house. A long time ago, back in the 19th century, a miller and his family lived in the original part of the house. It was just a little cottage then. Their daughter was only about your age, and a normal happy girl. But one day, so the story goes, they found her in her room, tearing at the wall with her bare hands, screaming with terror. She had smashed her mirror, and she was standing on the broken glass without even noticing, cutting her little feet to shreds.

JAMIE   That's gross Mr Barness.

MR BARNESS   That's not all Jamie. She said there were people in the mirror, and people in the walls. She said they were trying to hurt her.

JAMIE   Why didn't they just move house?

MR BARNESS   They did. But there's more. My great-grandfather fought in the First World War, all the young men from round here did. His best friend lived next door, with his parents and his younger brother and sister. One day both children were found drowned in the river. It turned out that on that very same day, my great-grandfather's best friend was killed in action. Then twenty years ago, Emily Parfitt drowned too. Now your sister.

JAMIE   But Lorna's alright Mr Barness. She didn't die.

*Cut back to **Lorna** and **Chris**.*

LORNA   Chris ...!

CHRIS   I'm sorry, I thought you wanted me to.

LORNA   No, I'm glad – I mean I did want you to, it's just that I … you surprised me, I guess.

CHRIS   Lorna, I just came to say goodbye.

LORNA   What? What the hell is that supposed to mean?

CHRIS   I'm leaving.

LORNA   What? When?

CHRIS   Today.

LORNA   But you just got here. Where are you going?

CHRIS   I can't tell you.

LORNA   What do you mean 'I can't tell you?' You're not in the CIA you know.

CHRIS   Lorna I …

LORNA   Why do you have to go?

CHRIS   I just do. Look, I don't mean to upset you, I just came to say goodbye. I really have to go. I'm sorry.

LORNA   Wait. You can't leave now. I need you. How can I contact you?

CHRIS   You can't.

LORNA   What?

CHRIS   You can't Lorna.

LORNA   So that's it? No explanation? You're just going to leave?

CHRIS   I'm sorry Lorna, that's just the way it is.

LORNA   Don't say, 'that's just the way it is' like I'm supposed to understand.

CHRIS   Lorna I …

LORNA   Just go Chris, I don't bloody care.

*He turns to go. Cut back to **Jamie** and **Mr Barness**.*

MR BARNESS	I know she's alright Jamie. But for how long? I'm telling you this because I'm worried about Lorna. What happened to her is exactly like what happened to young Emily.
JAMIE	I don't get it Mr Barness.
MR BARNESS	Emily said she was haunted by voices and visions. Everyone thought she was going mad.
JAMIE	How do you know all this?
MR BARNESS	This is a small town Jamie. And people are saying the same things about your sister.
JAMIE	Well I don't care what people are saying. Lorna's fine!
MR BARNESS	I don't mean to upset you Jamie. I don't think Lorna's going mad. It's not the people; it's the house, or something in it. We all hear things in our heads that other people can't hear. We all hear voices. They are a warning Jamie. A sign that something isn't right. And something isn't right Jamie. Something isn't right with that house.
JAMIE	I still don't understand.
MR BARNESS	Some things aren't meant to be understood. Sometimes things just are.
JAMIE	Look, thanks a lot Mr Barness, but I think I should probably be getting home now. My Mum gets worried.
MR BARNESS	Alright Jamie, give my best to Lorna.
JAMIE	I will. Bye.
	*Cut back to **Lorna** and **Chris**.*
LORNA	Wait! Don't go.
CHRIS	I'm glad you're OK. Really glad.
LORNA	But I thought we were friends – more than friends, I thought you cared about me.
CHRIS	I do care Lorna. More than you know. I'll miss you.

LORNA   No. Please Chris, don't leave me.

He pauses.

CHRIS   I have to Lorna. You've got to believe me when I say
I'd stay if I could. But I have no choice.

LORNA   No Chris, wait. Let me come with you.

CHRIS   What? No, you don't know what you're saying.

LORNA   Then why don't you explain it to me!

CHRIS   I can't, I told you. I don't expect you to understand.

LORNA   Then I don't have to. All I know is that I don't want to
lose you like I lost my family.

CHRIS   Lorna I … I just don't know.

LORNA   Take me with you Chris, please.

CHRIS   Lorna, what you're asking … I can't explain it to you,
but it means leaving everything. For you to come with
me you have to leave everything behind you and come
with me now.

LORNA   But why?

CHRIS   Because it's the only way Lorna. The only way we can
be together.

LORNA   Then let's do it. It's what I want. You do want me to
come with you, don't you?

CHRIS   Yes. I do. Come with me Lorna.

Lorna hugs him.

CHRIS   You look tired.

LORNA   I am. Really tired.

CHRIS   You should get some rest.

LORNA   Chris. You won't leave will you?

CHRIS   Get some sleep. And when you wake up, I'll still be
here, and you won't be tired anymore.

*As **Lorna** drifts off to sleep, **Chris** walks over to the mirror.*

CHRIS She's coming with me now. You won't be able to hurt her anymore like you hurt Emily. You can't win this time. It's over.

Lights.

SCENE FOURTEEN LEAVING

*Jamie bursts into **Lorna's** room.*

JAMIE Lorna, I have to talk to you! You aren't going to believe this. Lorna, wake up, there's something I have to tell you. Lorna? Lorna wake up! No. Mum! Mum quick!

*Music. **Lorna** and **Chris**, hand in hand, walk past him and off, perhaps through the audience. As **Jamie** cradles **Lorna** (represented by the bedcloth) in his arms, the **Girl** appears in silhouette in the broken mirror, and as the lights fade, the music volume drops and we hear her voice once again.*

GIRL Jamie. Jamie…

Music fades up again.

THE END

ACTIVITIES

THINGS TO TALK ABOUT

1   *Walking with Shadows* is a fine example of a particular genre. That is, the play is a member of a family of stories and dramas that have similar characteristics while keeping their own individual identity. Talk about:

- other films, plays and novels you know which seem to be a part of this family;

- what sort of features seem to connect these different stories and the way they are told;

- what the 'individual' features of this particular play are, that is, what makes it different from other examples of the genre.

2   Although the play is called *Walking with Shadows* and there is a 'Shadow Chorus', we are never told exactly what the 'shadows' are or might represent. What do you think? Talk about:

- what different sorts of shadows seem to be present in the play;

- does the fact that the exact nature of the shadows remains a mystery add to the play? Or would you have liked a clear explanation with all the loose ends tied up?

3   *Walking With Shadows* could be described as a 'psychological thriller'.

- In what way did the play 'thrill' you? Pick out at least three moments that you think should make an audience tingle and try to say why you have chosen them.

- In what ways is the play concerned with psychology? Is it just Lorna Moon's psyche that is being explored, or does the play explore the way other people, including the audience, think and feel?

4 Although this is quite a spooky play and the ending is certainly dark, it also contains quite a lot of humour.

- Which bits of the play did you find funny?

- How does adding these lighter moments contribute to the overall dramatic effectiveness of the narrative?

5 At first, an audience may wonder if Lorna really is experiencing something supernatural rather than everything just being in her mind. However, the playwright starts to introduce a number of things which suggest that something strange really is going on. Pick out a number of instances which do this. At what point did you become convinced that she really was hearing/seeing things that were not just in her imagination?

6 Is Chris a 'goody' or a 'baddy'? Does he 'save' Lorna, or is he part of some sinister and supernatural game with the Girl?

7 The ending of this version of the play is quite different from the original. In fact, the author sketched out various endings to see which would be the most sinister. Perhaps achieving the ultimate sinister effect is impossible because different people are affected by different things. What other possible endings can you dream up and what effect would you hope to achieve with them?

THINGS TO WRITE ABOUT

8 Consider the way Lorna's relationship with her brother Jamie seems to change as the play moves on. Compare, for example, how she behaves towards him in Act One Scene 4, Act One Scene 15 and Act Two Scene 3. What do you suppose Jamie makes of what is happening to his sister?

- Write a series of short diary entries which would trace Jamie's perspective on his changing relationship with Lorna.

9 Think about the key elements of this play. What words could you use to describe it? Try to write just one paragraph that could be used to publicise a production of the play. Your aim is to entice an audience along to see the play without giving too much away about what actually happens.

10 At one point in the play, Lorna is desperately upset by a note that has been passed around her class. Perhaps this has happened to you too. (Or maybe you sometimes pass notes yourself!) Working in a small group, write a series of gossipy notes that might be passed around a classroom, then find a way of using them as a script for a scene. Don't use any other dialogue, just find a way of using what you've written.

11 What is the relationship between Chris and the Girl? Write another scene which would explain their relationship and why they seem to be in competition to 'win' Lorna.

BRINGING THE PLAY TO LIFE

12 The original cast of *Walking with Shadows* had a lot of fun working on the school scenes and Ben Myers used a lot of ideas generated in improvisations in his final script.

- In groups, choose any one of the school-based scenes which you particularly liked.

- Decide what the purpose of the scene is and note a few things that must happen or be said to achieve this.

- Now improvise the scene for yourself. You can add as many of your own lines as you please and introduce new characters. The aim though must be to make the scene feel realistic and lively while still getting the main points across to an audience.

13 The problem with having a number of characters with fairly small parts, such as the school pupils in this play, is that they can sometimes seem too bland and stereotyped. The challenge is to give each character, no matter how few lines they have, individual characteristics. There are a number of ways of achieving this:

- work in groups of four or five and give yourselves new character names;

- improvise a simple scene set in a school, For example, the group might be talking about an incident that has happened in class or the arrival of a new teacher;

- now try the scene again but this time each of you should slightly alter the way you normally speak by either going a little slower or faster and perhaps having a certain expression that you frequently use (it might be something as simple as 'Yeah!' or 'Know what I mean?');

- try it out again and this time adopt a particular way of standing and moving. Perhaps you might bounce a bit when you walk or always stand with your hands thrust deep into your pockets. The danger is going too far with all this which will simply make you look ridiculous! Try to be subtle;

- share your scene with the rest of the group and see if they can pick out the individual characteristics you have given to your characters.

14 After Lorna is rescued from the river she is admitted to hospital and meets Dr Lane, a psychiatrist. In pairs, improvise a series of short meetings between Dr Lane and Lorna in which the psychiatrist tries to understand what is happening to Lorna. From a psychiatrist's point of view, meetings such as these must be handled very carefully. Their aim is to help the patient feel comfortable enough to talk about whatever they want to talk about. This involves listening very carefully to the patient and then gently asking questions. It's a bit like peeling away the different layers of an onion to get to the heart of the matter. It takes time and perhaps in Lorna's case the 'truth' is never discovered.

Try to make your series of short scenes reflect the delicacy of the situation. Take your time. Choose your words carefully and see if you can build up a sense of mystery through your work.

15 Set out four chairs in different corners of the room. You will need four volunteers to sit on these seats and adopt the role of either Jamie, Mum, one of Lorna's best friends and one of her teachers. Move around each of these characters and hotseat them to find out what they think about Lorna as a person. After perhaps ten minutes of this, come together as a whole class and discuss how the different characters see Lorna.

STAGING THE PLAY

16 If they are not delivered well, some of the lines in *Walking with Shadows* could sound really cheesy! For example, lots of the ghostly girl's lines such as 'I have come for you' or 'I'm coming Lorna' might sound like extracts from *Scooby Doo* unless they are handled imaginatively.

Choose any one of the scenes involving Lorna and the Girl and experiment with different ways of making the scene chilling. You might try using positioning as well as different types of voice to achieve the best effect.

17 Playing the character of Chris represents quite a challenge to an actor. He could be described as 'enigmatic' (an enigma is a kind of puzzle). No one seems to know exactly who he is or where he has come from. At the end of the play we discover that there really is something strange about him.

- Look back through the script and note how we first get to hear about Chris.

- In groups, rehearse the Party scene (pages 27–30). What impression do you want the audience to have of Chris at this point? Both the actor playing Chris and the other characters in the scene need to try to find a way of suggesting that he is a bit special but what happens if you make him too obviously spooky?

- Now rehearse the scene in which Chris entices Lorna to go with him (pages 73–75) Can you find a way of making Chris appear more 'other-wordly' here?

18 A similar challenge faces the actors who will play the Shadow Chorus. Are they voices in Lorna's head? Or are they something else? What effect should they have on an audience?

- In groups, work on Act One Scene 1. Being the opening scene of the play it is important that an atmosphere is set up which will grip the audience and let them know just what sort of play they have come to see. You need to decide exactly what you want the audience to feel at the end of this scene then experiment with ways of using your voices and movements to achieve this.

- What sort of lighting and sound effects could you use to enhance the atmosphere of this opening sequence?

19 Ben Myers uses a number of interesting techniques in the play to make the staging of it interesting. For example, Act One Scene 2 is set in the school playground yet we also see and hear what happened in the art lesson. Similarly, in Act Two Scene 6 Lorna's conversation with the Shadow Chorus is inter-cut with a telephone conversation between her Mum and Dad.

- In groups, select one of these scenes and find a way of staging it so that the audience is clear about what is going on even though the action is set in different times and places.

20 Sound effects and music can help to add considerable tension to a drama. (Next time you watch a thriller or horror film pay attention to this. You may not have noticed before just how much background music actually occurs in such films.)

- Pick out at least three moments in the play where you think a piece of music could help build the tension. What sort of music would you choose?

- One device that can be helpful is to have a particular sound effect which is used as a 'motif' for a character. In other words, every time that character appears, or is about to appear, the audience hears the same effect. This sort of motif might be quite simple. Try using just one or two instruments (a triangle, guitar or perhaps a synthesiser) to create a motif for Chris and the Girl.

21 In the original production of *Walking with Shadows*, screens were used to show certain characters such as Mum and Dad in silhouette only. The screens were made of thin gauze and lit from behind.

- In groups, rehearse Act One Scene 8 (pages 31–33) in a way that doesn't have Mum and Dad clearly visible on stage and talk about the effect this has on the way this might change an audience's understanding of Lorna's relationship with her parents.

- Which other adult characters do you think might also be presented on stage in the same way? What dramatic effect would you hope to achieve by using this technique with them?

22 Another interesting technique used in the original production was the projection of film clips. This was particularly effective in building up the tension in Act Two Scene 10 (pages 67–68) where Lorna is pulled towards the river.

- Make up a simple 'storyboard' to show what different images you could project in sequence to build up the tension in this scene.

- Pick another moment in the play when you think it would be dramatically effective to project a series of either still or moving images.

STRANGER THAN FICTION

Do you believe in ghosts? Whether you do or not, there is no denying that in every known human culture there are stories and traditions surrounding the idea of some sort of spirit world. Ghosts are said to be the spirits of people who for some reason refuse to leave the world of the living after their mortal existence has ended. There are countless stories of ghostly encounters, mountains of books about recorded sightings and literally hundreds of websites devoted to the topic. The whole subject of ghosts and spirits calls into question what we mean by 'facts'. Certainly, there have been plenty of strange things happen that can not be explained by our current understanding, but does that prove the existence of ghosts? Maybe there are other explanations that we simply haven't come up with yet.

One thing that has been noticed though is that a particular kind of spirit does seem to be attracted to teenage girls. *Poltergeist* is the name given to a destructive 'spirit'. *Poltern* is the German word for 'knock' and *geist*, obviously, means 'ghost'. These spirits characteristically make a lot of noise and have been known not only to move furniture but even to cause things to be flung across the room. In many recorded cases their appearance seems to be linked with the presence of a young teenage girl suffering from psychological or emotional stress. Sometimes it is discovered that the girl herself is consciously or unconsciously causing the destruction but this explanation does not seem to explain all cases. Even so, some researchers think that these strange occurrences are evidence of the immense power of the human mind rather than anything to do with things from another dimension.

23 What do you think a ghost is? Conduct a debate in your class around the question 'Do ghosts really exist?' One way of keeping such a debate in order (and they can get pretty heated, so be warned!) is to keep to one strict rule. That is, speakers for and against the notion must take it in turns so that if one person argues for the case, the next speaker must argue against and so on.

24 What ghost stories exist in your area? Either your school or local library is almost certain to have collections of local ghost stories and perhaps you know some of them already. The Watermill Theatre in Newbury where *Walking with Shadows* was first produced is reputed to be haunted by a young girl whom it is thought may have been killed by the machinery there when it was a corn mill. She appears in one of the upper rooms in the building and theatre staff refuse to go there alone!

- In small groups, take it in turns to tell the same story in two different ways. On the first telling, your aim is to really convince the audience that something genuinely strange and perhaps sinister has taken place. In the second telling your aim should be to try to provide a completely logical and rational explanation for what has occurred. Talk about the different ways people use their voices, choice of words and facial expressions to achieve these different aims.

- Research into local stories and use your findings as the basis of a written story or short play of your own.

Further work

What would it be like to be lost somewhere between the world as we know it and some other place? J. M. Barrie explored this question in a number of his plays. You will probably already know his story *Peter Pan*. While you may have always thought of this as a simple children's story, there is a darker side to it. When Barrie was aged six, his elder brother was killed in a skating accident. He later wrote. 'When I became a man, he was still a boy of thirteen'. The idea of children staying children forever because they died young is reflected in both the character of Peter Pan and the Lost Boys he lives with in Never Never Land. Perhaps he is also suggesting that when we grow up we lose touch with an important part of ourselves. Peter Pan loses touch with his shadow and maybe it is that that keeps him a boy; as we get older our own personal shadow gets bigger both literally and metaphorically.

This idea seems to have bothered J. M. Barrie a great deal and he explored it further in a very disturbing play called *Mary Rose*. The story involves a young girl, Mary Rose, who mysteriously disappears for three weeks while visiting an uninhabited Scottish island. Mary grows up, gets married and returns to the island with her husband and baby son. She disappears again, this time, apparently, for good. Years later though she returns but by this time her baby has grown up and gone to sea. The play ends when her son returns to the now deserted house where he was a child and meets the ghost of Mary Rose who is still lost in some strange in-between world:

HARRY   Come to me ghostie; I wish you would.

MARY ROSE   Certainly not.

HARRY   If you come, I'll try to help you.

She goes at once and sits on his knee.

See here, when I was sitting by the fire alone I seemed to hear you as you once were saying that some day when he was a man you would like to sit on your Harry's knee.

MARY ROSE   The loveliest time of all will be when he is a man and takes me on his knee instead of my taking him on mine.

HARRY   Do you see who I am now?

MARY ROSE   Nice man.

HARRY   Is that all you know about me?

MARY ROSE   Yes.

HARRY   Poor soul, I wonder if there was ever a man with a ghost on his knee before.

MARY ROSE   I don't know.

HARRY   Seems to me you're feared of being a ghost. I dare say, to a timid thing, being a ghost is worse than seeing them.

MARY ROSE   Yes.

HARRY   Is it lonely being a ghost?

MARY ROSE   Yes.

HARRY   Do you know any other ghost?

MARY ROSE   No.

HARRY   Would you like to know other ghosts?

MARY ROSE   Yes.

HARRY   I can understand that. And now would you like to go away and play?

MARY ROSE   Please.

HARRY   In this cold house, when you should be searching, do you sometimes play by yourself instead?

MARY ROSE *(Whispering.)* Don't tell.

(From *Mary Rose* by J. M. Barrie, Oxford University Press.)

25 Mary Rose is Harry's mother but she doesn't know he is her son. Why doesn't he tell her?

- In groups of three, rehearse this scene with one of you acting as a director. Try to find a way of showing Mary Rose's innocence and set this against Harry's sympathy for her.

- It's an odd situation here isn't it? Both characters are rather lost and lonely. Try to bring out this sadness in the way you play the scene.

26 Use the idea of people somehow becoming lost in a parallel world for a scene of your own devising. What is that world like? Why might it be the case that being a ghost is more terrifying than seeing one?